THE MIRACLE OF
HOPE

Books by Charles L. Allen

Roads to Radiant Living
In Quest of God's Power
God's Psychiatry
When the Heart is Hungry
The Touch of the Master's Hand
All Things Are Possible Through Prayer
When You Lose a Loved One
The Twenty-Third Psalm
Twelve Ways to Solve Your Problem
Healing Words
The Life of Christ
The Lord's Prayer
Prayer Changes Things
The Ten Commandments
The Sermon on the Mount
The Beatitudes
Life More Abundant
The Charles L. Allen Treasury
When You Graduate
The Miracle of Love
The Miracle of Hope

THE MIRACLE OF
HOPE

CHARLES L. ALLEN

Fleming H. Revell Company
Old Tappan, New Jersey

Unless indicated otherwise, all Scripture quotations in this volume are from the King James Version of the Bible.

Scripture quotations identified RSV are from the Revised Standard Version of the Bible, Copyrighted 1946 and 1952.

Scripture quotation identified MOFFATT is from The Bible: A New Translation by James Moffatt, Copyright, 1954 by James Moffatt. By permission of Harper & Row, Publishers, Inc.

Quotation from *The Cocktail Party* by T. S. Eliot is used by permission of the publishers, Harcourt Brace Jovanovich, Inc.

Quotation from *Orpheus Descending* by Tennessee Williams, Copyright 1955, © 1958 by Tennessee Williams, Reprinted by permission of New Directions Publishing Corporation.

Material about Arthur Gordon is based on his article which appeared in *Reader's Digest*, January, 1960, © 1959 by Reader's Digest Association, Inc., Pleasantville, N.Y.

Quotation by Tom Landry is from "Why Is This Man Laughing?" by Edwin Shrake, *Sports Illustrated*, September 18, 1972, © 1972.

Diligent effort has been made to locate and secure permission for the inclusion of all copyrighted material in this book. If any such acknowledgments have been omitted, the publishers would appreciate receiving full information so that proper credit may be given in future editions.

Allen, Charles Livingstone   Date/
      The miracle of hope.

        1. Hope—Meditations. I. Title.
BVD638.A56   234'.2   73-9812
ISBN 0-8007-0609-9

Copyright © 1973 Fleming H. Revell Company
All rights reserved
Printed in the United States of America

TO my grandchildren

Charles L. Allen III
Jack deMange Allen
Margaret Ann Allen
Charles William Miller, Jr.
Carolyn Kay Miller
John O'Brien Miller
John Franklin Allen, Jr.

They give me hope for the future

Contents

Preface

While there's life there's hope.

MIGUEL DE CERVANTES, *Don Quixote*

Hope is like the sun, which, as we journey towards it, casts the shadow of our burden behind us.

SAMUEL SMILES, *Self-Help*

It is worth a thousand pounds a year to have the habit of looking on the bright side of things.

SAMUEL JOHNSON

The mighty hopes that make us men.

ALFRED, LORD TENNYSON, *In Memoriam*

In these pages I lift up some of the great affirmations of hope from the Bible which have blessed my own heart and made my own days brighter. I have purposely kept this book on hope brief that one might more easily take hold of it and make hope a surer possession of his own. The joy of hope is my prayer for you.

CHARLES L. ALLEN
First United Methodist Church
Houston, Texas

Introduction

Some years ago, one of our nation's submarines sank off the coast of Massachusetts, becoming a prison for its crew. Ships were rushed to the scene and divers went down to see if anything could be done. The men in the submarine clung desperately to life as slowly their oxygen supply was exhausted. The divers and the men inside communicated with each other by tapping dots and dashes of the Morse code. Time was running out and after a seemingly long pause, a question was slowly tapped out from inside the submarine: "Is...there... any ... hope?"

"Is there any hope?" is a question that has been or will be in the heart of every person at some point in life. Most likely the agony of that question will be experienced not just once, but many times. The Psalmist cries, "Why art thou cast down, O my soul? and why art thou disquieted within me?" (Psalms 42:11). Again in the very next psalm, the same question in the same words is repeated. In truth, these words are spoken again and again.

1.

Hope deferred maketh the heart sick.

Look through the eyes of John's Gospel at those people gathered about the pool at Bethesda. It is a wretched sight. There "lay a great multitude of impotent folk, of blind, halt, withered . . ." (John 5:3). It was the gathering place for those of that city who were crippled, sick, blind, helpless, and friendless. It comes as no surprise to read that Jesus was there, also. He seemed to always be where there was someone in need.

These people were not without hope. They believed that an angel came at certain times and troubled the water. The first one to step into the pool after the troubling of the water would be healed. Jesus fixed His eyes on one man who had been there for thirty-eight years. What a marvelous hope that man had! The Bible tells us that "Hope deferred maketh the heart sick. " Imagine a hope that can live for thirty-eight years! Some people lose hope at their very first disappointment.

Deferred hope is truly no respector of persons. In the very community in which each of us lives, there are numerous people to gather about our own town's Bethesda pool. There are those who live in the "lower end" of the city—the winos, alcoholics, dope addicts,

13

prostitutes, and the disinherited. Many of these are too sick to hope any longer.

Just a little way up the street we find the economically poor, the racial minorities, and the uneducated. Many are still hoping that a busy, fluent society will accord them the privilege of being accepted as human beings.

Go into every section of the town and there are people sickened by deferred hope. Many have learned that one can be lonely in a crowd. They have learned that loneliness is different from aloneness or solitude. Loneliness is the feeling of being left out from others. How many are there who have turned away from an empty mailbox after the postman has gone by, or sat by a phone waiting for it to ring, or listened for a knock on the door that is delayed day after day after day?

Hope deferred—there are those who are sick, hoping for a cure to be discovered. Others have kept hoping for word about a loved one lost in action in some war. The list of those holding hopes which are deferred is endless. In fact, in many the hope has faded out and in its place has come to live despair, or disappointment, or bitterness, or any other member of the family of hopelessness. Hope can die.

2.
But we had hoped that he was the
one to redeem Israel.

On the afternoon of the day of our Lord's Resurrection, He saw two sad people walking along the road from Jerusalem to Emmaus. Unrecognized, Jesus fell in step with them and they talked as they went along together. Thinking their traveling companion was a stranger who did not know what had happened, they explained who Jesus was and how He had been crucified.

Then they said with sorrow, "But we had hoped that he was the one to redeem Israel." We note that their hope is past tense. Here is hope that is dead—"We had hoped."

God gave man the capacity to hope—to dream—to see beyond what is to what might be.

> For man is dreaming ever,
>   He glimpses the hills afar,
> And plans for the things out yonder
>   Where all his tomorrows are:
> And back of the sound of the hammer,
>   And back of the hissing steam,

And back of the hand on the throttle,
Is ever a daring dream.

AUTHOR UNKNOWN

But sometimes dreams do not become reality. The great and beloved preacher, Dr. J. Wallace Hamilton, has a chapter entitled "Shattered Dreams" in his book *Horns and Halos in Human Nature.* He tells of the weirdest auction sale in history. It was held in the city of Washington in 1926. One hundred fifty thousand patent models of old inventions were declared obsolete and put up for sale. The people would laugh as things were put up, such as a bedbug buster and an illuminated cat to scare away mice. There was a gadget which enabled a mother to churn the milk and rock the baby in one operation. There was a device to prevent snoring which consisted of a trumpet reaching from the mouth to the ear. It was designed to awaken the snorer instead of the neighbors. One man invented a tube to reach from his mouth to his feet so his breath would keep his feet warm while he slept. There was an adjustable pulpit which could be raised or lowered. The auctioneer told how a preacher in Ohio was preaching on the subject "Where Will You Spend Eternity?" During his sermon he accidentally hit the button on the pulpit and down he went.

That auction of old patent models was good for 150,000 laughs. But look deeper and we see it also represented 150,000 broken dreams. Somebody had high hopes for each of those inventions. Long hours of work were put into each one of them. Many hoped for fame and fortune to result. Some died in poverty trying to sell what they had invented. One hundred fifty thousand dead hopes!

In His most beloved story, Jesus told of the young man who "gathered all together, and took his journey into a far country..." (Luke 15:13). He envisioned an exciting and good life, a time of freedom and joy. In some form or another, this dream has possessed the minds of great numbers of people. Many believe that out yonder somewhere, away from the restraint of day, is true happiness. It is a high hope which sends many out. The prodical son ended up at a hog trough. His hopes were shattered.

There among the hogs he seized upon a new hope. "How many hired servants of my father's have bread enough and to spare ... I will arise and go to my father..." (Luke 15:17,18). Hope died but a new hope was born.

A good example of how one can start again after seemingly total defeat comes out of the life of Thomas Carlyle. There was a period in his life when he was living in almost total poverty and defeat. During this time he labored to write the first volume of the history of the French Revolution. It was his greatest work and he felt it would bring to him the literary success he sought. When he had finally completed the first volume, he took it to John Stuart Mill to read. Mill sat by his fire and carefully read the remarkable work page by page. One morning his maid was cleaning the room and, seeing the disarrayed pages of the manuscript on the floor by Mill's chair, she thought they were papers he had discarded so she used them to build a fire.

When Carlyle learned that the work into which he had put so much was destroyed, he was a depressed and defeated man. He had neither the strength nor the heart to start over. He vowed he would never write again. For days and days he brooded over his misfortune. Then one day he looked out the window and saw a man building a brick wall. He watched as the man picked up one brick at a time and set it in place.

As Carlyle watched, he decided he would write his book again, by writing one page at a time. So it was that the hope which had died began to live again.

3.
I hope to see you in passing
as I go to Spain.

Saint Paul was writing to the Romans. He told them that he hoped to see them on his way to Spain. Going to Spain was his great dream, his high hope. But Paul never got to Spain. Instead, a prison cell in Rome was where his journey ended. It has been well said that every man dreams of one life and is forced to live another. Many "die with all their music in them," as Oliver Wendell Holmes said, but many learn to sing again. Out of frustrations, disappointments, and dead hopes can come new life. One of the lessons we learn as we read biographies is that very few get to live life on the basis of his or her first choice. Most persons have to settle for a second or third choice.

Some years ago I went to Enterprise, Alabama, to speak. In the center of the town I saw the strangest monument I have ever seen. It is a goddess on a lighted pedestal holding aloft a giant boll weevil. As we all know, the boll weevil is the deadly enemy of cotton. This insect swept across the South and impoverished the farmers. My first thought was that these people had put on that pedestal their great enemy to remind themselves to keep on hating him. But not so. On the base of the monument is this inscription: **In profound appreciation of the boll weevil, and what it has done as the herald of prosperity, this monument was erected by the citizens of Enterprise, Coffee County, Alabama.**

I inquired and learned the story. In the year 1919, the boll weevil came and destroyed the cotton crops. The area was dependent on cotton and this was a great calamity. At that time the people had almost no way to fight the new enemy. They seemed to be facing a hopeless situation. But somebody tried planting peanuts and it was discovered that the climate and soil in that area were ideally suited for peanuts. This area became the peanut-growing capital of the world and the people became more prosperous than they had ever been. Out of a tragedy a new hope came.

The story comes to mind of that night when the disciples of Jesus were caught in a storm at sea. The waves beat over the sides of the ship until it was almost filled with water. It appeared that sinking was imminent. They had done their best but they could not cope with the storm. Many people have had this very experience. They have been overcome by circumstances beyond their control. There come times when it is hard to keep on hoping.

Jesus was asleep in the stern of the ship. The disciples woke Him up and said, "Master, carest thou not that we perish?" (Mark 4:38). They were not the last ones to wonder if God cares. Sometimes in seeming hopelessness we can believe that we are forgotten, even by God. But Jesus rose and said, "Peace, be still" (verse 39). The wind ceased and the sea became calm. Then He said to the disciples, "Why are ye so fearful? how is it that ye have no faith?" (verse 40). The disciples said to each other, "What manner of man is this, that even the wind and the sea obey him?" (verse 41). Out of a seemingly hopeless situation they gained a new faith.

I have often remembered a sentence from Lloyd C. Douglas's book *White Banners* —"sometimes a disappointment closes a door in a person's face, and then he looks about for some other door, and opens it, and gets something better than he had been hunting for the first time."

Not every failure turns into blessing. Not every sorrow brings out the sunshine of life. Not every prison opens into glorious service. Some people are forced to live out the balance of their years with a broken body, a broken home, a broken heart. But listen to the testimony of Saint Paul:

> ". . . five times received I forty stripes save one. Thrice was I beaten with rods, once was I stoned, thrice I suffered shipwreck, a night and a day I have been in the deep. In journeyings often, in perils of waters, in perils of robbers, in perils by mine own

countrymen, in perils by the heathen, in perils in the
city, in perils in the wilderness, in perils in the sea,
in perils among false brethren; In weariness and
painfulness, in watchings often, in hunger and thirst,
in fastings often, in cold and nakedness.

2 Corinthians 11:24-27

What a list of hurting, disappointing, frightening experiences! But through his trials he carried a bright hope
and was able to write to the Romans, as Dr. Moffatt
beautifully translates it, "No one who believes in him. . .
will ever be disappointed. . . . No one" (Romans 10:11
MOFFATT).

4.

We are saved by hope.

Hanging in the Tate Gallery in London is George Frederic Watts's great painting entitled *Hope*. It pictures a blindfolded woman sitting on the world, stricken and dejected. In her hand is a harp with all the strings broken except one. She is striking that one string and her head is bent toward it in closest attention to catch its sound. This is the artist's picture of hope, triumphant over the world's sin and sorrow, triumphant over anything and everything that can hurt a human being. When all else is gone, one still has hope left and hope can triumph.

There are many stories of people who were inspired by Watts's painting. One that I like tells of a man who was on his way to drown himself. On the way he saw this painting in a store window. He looked carefully at the blindfolded woman on her world of misery, playing on the one string. Finally he said, "Well, I have one string —I have a little boy at home," and he retraced his steps.

In one form or another, that story can be repeated countless times. No matter how bad life is, if one will only look, he can always find one hope that is left and that one hope can be the saving power.

Life can weigh heavily on a person and can eventually

break one down. Another painting which comes to mind is Jean Francois Millet's *Man With Hoe*. Some believe the French artist intended to show the dignity of labor. Others see the painting as showing one who is weary, crushed, and defeated. Look at the painting and you see a man leaning upon his hoe. That hoe is the heaviest-looking hoe one can imagine.

Edwin Markham saw Millet's painting and was moved to write:

> Bowed by the weight of centuries he leans
>> Upon his hoe and gazes on the ground,
> The emptiness of ages in his face,
>> And on his back the burden of the world.

Add just one little letter of the alphabet to that phrase and instead of "Man with hoe," you get "Man with hope." What a difference it makes to change "hoe" to "hope." We certainly would not eliminate hoes from the world. The hoe represents labor and labor is of God. Sometimes we feel that life would be wonderful if we could give up our jobs and live in ease and comfort. It is not so. Someone has quoted Michelangelo, the great Italian sculptor, as saying, "It is only well with me when I have a chisel in my hand."

We are glad that men do have hoes and that we have opportunity to use our hoes. Unemployment is always a haunting horror. A painting of a man *without* a hoe would be worse—much worse. But along with his hoe, man also needs a hope. There is an old slave song of protest and escape—

> Hang up the shovel and the hoe,
> Take down the fiddle and the bow.

This is not the answer. Every man needs his hoe—his work. The hoe is not a hopeless instrument. It is quite the contrary. The man in the field with his hoe is looking toward a harvest, a harvest that will feed and clothe him and his loved ones. The man with the hoe has a reward to look forward to. Hoe and hope go hand in hand. It is when the man loses his hope that he "leans upon his hoe and gazes on the ground." Hoes are not made for leaning on. A hoe is for hoeing and the hope of the harvest is what makes all the difference.

The world's salvation will not be found in some great hoe-dropping movement. No one ever finds life's greatest happiness through escape.

Andrew Carnegie was fond of saying, "Three generations from shirtsleeves to shirtsleeves." What this means is that children of rich men have a hard time finding the moral equivalent of the struggles through which their fathers obtained their wealth. Man is not born to be satisfied. When man is satisfied he becomes bored and boredom leads to self-destruction. We are made strong by the struggle. Look at the lives of the early pioneers who faced harsh climates, sparse land, and endless toil. Out of their efforts came a sturdy civilization. The unfriendly environment could not defeat them because in them was the hope of that civilization they were building.

There was a man named Henry P. Crowell who had tuberculosis. In his day there was no cure for this dreaded disease and he was making his way west to die. The slow train he was on stopped at a station where nearby was a grain mill with a FOR SALE sign on it. He got off the train, bought the mill, and set to work to get it going again. That was the beginning of Quaker Oats. He made a fortune, overcame his tuberculosis, and lived past the age of ninety.

Sir Thomas Buxton said a wonderful thing:

> The longer I live the more deeply I am convinced that that which makes the difference between one man and another—between the weak and the powerful, the great and insignificant, is energy—invisible determination—a purpose once formed and then death or victory. This quality will do anything that has to be done in the world; and no talents, no circumstances, no opportunities will make one a man without it.

Underscore that phrase—"a purpose once formed and then death or victory." That breeds hope that saves.

Saint Paul based his declaration "We are saved by hope" (Romans 8:24) on two great truths. He started with a conviction that we are sons of God. He said, "For as many as are led by the Spirit of God, they are the sons of God" (Romans 8:14). Study man and you see he does not aimlessly drift through life. Man is a creature that is led. He has incentives which are beyond his physical self. Man is both physical and spiritual. If one lives just in the physical, is guided and controlled just by physical appetites and desires, he has none of life's great inspirations and incentives. If man is willing to be led by the Spirit of God, then he receives vision far beyond the mere physical. His spirit becomes stronger than his body and therein he finds power and salvation.

Then, following his declaration that we are saved by hope, Saint Paul affirms, "And we know that all things work together for good to them that love God, to them who are the called according to his purpose" (Romans 8:28). Here is a firm basis for hope. He does not say everything that happens is good. A lot of things that happen are not good. He believes that if man will consider all the experiences of his life, both the good and the bad, and cement them together with his love for God, then the sum total of his life will be good. That is, no matter what happens, keep on loving God and life will work out well. That is the basis of the hope that saves.

5.

. . . but we glory in tribulations also:
knowing that tribulation worketh patience;
And patience, experience; and experience, hope.

Tribulation—patience—experience—hope. That is the order in which it comes. If man never had trouble, he would never have any hope. Troubles develop patience which enables man to bear life as he goes on living. And as man lives he gains experience. As a result of experience in living, man can and does see reason for hope. If we could not look back and see victories gained over adverse circumstances, we would have no hope in the midst of the troubles we are experiencing today, or fear that we might experience tomorrow.

"It is history that teaches us to hope," said Robert E. Lee. That is absolutely true, whether we are seeing history as related to the world and all people or whether we are looking at history just in reference to our own lives. Memory is a great producer of hope.

Dr. Norman Vincent Peale has proclaimed the message of hope to numberless multitudes of people. He is one of my finest inspirations and one of the ministers to whom I personally owe the most. In 1960 he preached a sermon entitled "Why We Say Merry Christmas." In that sermon he told about an article by Arthur Gordon which appeared in *Reader's Digest.* Arthur Gordon experienced a dry period in his writing. His thoughts did not flow as they once had; he found difficulty in saying what he wanted to say. He felt neither inspiration nor creative ability. After struggling for a period of time, he consulted a loved family physician who was wise and mature.

After hearing Arthur Gordon's story, the doctor said, "Life has gone out of you? Is that so?" And he asked him, "When you were a child what did you like to do most? What gave you the greatest joy?"

Gordon replied that he had enjoyed going to the beach and listening to the waves and the sea gulls.

"All right," said the doctor, "you spend the whole day tomorrow at the beach—alone. Get there at nine in the morning and stay until six at night. Take no writing materials, no books or other reading materials, no radio.

"Now," he continued, "I am going to give you four prescriptions." He took four pages off his pad, wrote something on each of them, numbered them, and said, "Take this one at nine o'clock, number two at twelve o'clock, number three at three o'clock, and number four at six o'clock."

The next day Arthur Gordon went to the beach. He sat for a moment in his car feeling futile and foolish. Then he read prescription number one: "Listen intently."

He got out of his car and walked up and down the beach for three hours, listening to the sounds that were there—the wind, the sea, the gulls.

A ter three hours of intent listening he took out the second prescription: "Try reaching back." He sat down between two sand dunes and tried reaching back in his memory, remembering happy experiences and high points of his life.

After three hours of remembering, he opened the third prescription which said, "Reexamine your motives." He asked himself why he wanted to write—to see his name in print? To make a lot of money? Or did he write because he wanted to help people? For three hours he reexamined his motives.

Then at six o'clock he turned to the fourth prescription which was, "Write your worries in the sand." He took a stick and wrote his worries. He walked away but he looked back and saw the tide come in and wash away what he had written. He felt clean and renewed.

In the year 1860, Elizabeth Akers Allen, writing under the pen name of Florence Percy, sent a poem entitled "Rock Me to Sleep" to the *Saturday Evening Post*, in which she expressed this longing to remember. Her words have been caught up by many, many people in the years since. She said:

> Backward, turn backward, O Time, in your flight,
> Make me a child again, just for to-night!

Through the process of memory we can become children again and it can be an experience which can re-create hope.

One of my best friends is an official of a large company. He had developed a drinking problem and with that, other problems had come. He had about reached the point of despair and hopelessness. He decided to take some days off. He drove a hundred miles to a rural community where his aged mother still lived at his old home. He slept in the bed where he had slept as a boy. He ate, at the kitchen table, the meals his mother fixed, just like he used to do. He took long walks in the field where he used to work as a farm boy.

Gradually his thoughts became the thoughts which had possessed him as a youth. He thought of the big world and how he wanted to be a part of it. He dreamed, like he used to, of becoming a man people would respect and who would make a contribution to the world. He began to believe in himself again. He remembered his early ambitions. He kept telling himself how he once walked away from those fields and accomplished his dreams and that now he could do it again. He captured a new hope and a new life.

My father used to preach a sermon on the text "And Peter remembered . . ." (Luke 22:61). The title of his sermon was "The Memory That Saves."

Not long ago I went to preach again in one of the

little churches where I started my ministry. It is located back in the mountains. The paved road ended at a sawmill about three miles from the church. Many cold winter mornings I parked my car at that sawmill and walked over the ice-covered dirt road to the church. The day I was back visiting, I stopped again at that sawmill and let my mind go back. As I sat there I kept asking myself the question "Why was I willing to walk through the cold snow and ice to that little church?" Not because of what they paid me, because in those depression years they paid me almost nothing. Not because of the crowds of people who would be there, because there were never more than a dozen or so who came. Not because of any recognition I would receive. I kept remembering why I did go. That memory encourages and strengthens me now.

"Tribulation—patience—experience—hope." Not only in reference to our own personal experiences, but also when we think of the lessons of history, this formula works. It is a discouraging experience to look at all the problems and troubles of the world. "But no man who is correctly informed as to the past," said Thomas Macaulay, "will be disposed to take a morose or desponding view of the present."

As we study history we learn that the pathway of mankind has not been easy. There have been dark periods of war and economic depression. There have been storms and earthquakes and major catastrophies of all kinds. Diseases and hunger have sent so many to early graves. But in spite of everything that has happened, the record of mankind is one of progress. Out of each setback has come a new beginning and a powerful forward surge.

In times of crises there is a tendency to lose hope for the future. There are always those who are preaching the end of civilization. History teaches us that the world is not doomed, that there is still progress to be made and we are challenged by the promise of a better world ahead. John Greenleaf Whittier looked at history and was inspired to write:

> And, step by step, since time began,
> I see the steady gain of man.

In a message to Congress in 1941, Franklin D. Roosevelt looked toward a future which would be secured by four essential freedoms. The freedom of speech and expression is the first. The second is the freedom of every person to worship God in his own way. The third is freedom from want and the fourth is freedom from fear. The proclamation of those four freedoms gave new hope to people who had just come through the agonies of the most destructive war the world had ever known.

The writer of Ecclesiastes said a long time ago, "Say not, 'Why were the former days better than these?'

For it is not from wisdom that you ask this" (7:10 RSV).
As we go back in memory to our own experiences and
as we look at mankind's life, we find our hopes
strengthened for both today and tomorrow.

In 1968 the Dallas Cowboys football team lost the
championship game to the Cleveland Browns. It was a
bitterly disappointing defeat. Speaking about that game,
Tom Landry made some wise observations. He said
in *Sports Illustrated:*

> Anyhow, that game and the one we lost to the
> Browns in the same playoffs the next year brought us
> a great deal of criticism. It may sound funny, but
> those games also helped us develop character as a
> team. When you lose the way we did, you can either
> come back disorganized, or you can come back and
> win again. No team could come back as we did after
> our 1970 shutout loss to St. Louis if we hadn't had
> the experience we had against Cleveland those two
> years and the great disappointment of the ice game
> against Green Bay in 1967. You can't turn yourself
> around if you don't have a backlog of adversity. The
> Apostle Paul says suffering brings on endurance,
> endurance brings character and character brings hope.
> Once you develop character you tend to always hope
> things will work out. The guy with character continues
> to do the best he can, even against the odds, and
> keeps a bright outlook.

Endicott Peabody, the famous headmaster of Groton School, summed it all up when he said to remember that things in life will not always run smoothly. Sometimes we will be rising toward the heights—then all will seem to reverse itself and start downward. The great fact to remember is that the trend of civilization itself is forever upward; that a line drawn through the middle of the peaks and the valleys of the centuries always has an upward trend.

That fact—and it *is* fact— is always cause for hope.

6.

That they might set their hope in God,
and not forget the works of God,
but keep his commandments.

Here we have memory, hope, and effort included together. The Psalmist is saying that God gave deliverance to His people. The remembering of that deliverance gives hope for the present. That hope brings inspiration to live for God in the future.

Living in a city can be a discouraging experience because we are confronted with so many problems. There are sections where the housing is inadequate and the people are poor. There are streets where it is dangerous to walk because of crime. Many people in the city are sick. There are those who are friendless and lonely, others who are discouraged and frustrated. In a city there are murders, rapes, automobile wrecks, and fires. There is polluted air. Every day people are buried who are dear to someone's heart. There is deep sorrow in the hearts of many people in every city. At times one feels a sense of hopelessness.

Many times during a year I drive out to the airport of my city and get on a plane. As the plane gains altitude I look out the window and see the city stretched below. It is a beautiful sight, especially at night when all the lights of the city are shining. From the airplane one gets a much more satisfying view of the city than when one is making his way through the narrow streets. Even though there are problems in the city, from the heights one sees the beauty and majesty of the city and is inspired by it.

So it is with life. Living in the present, one is constantly confronted with the trials and troubles of life. But when one looks back at life through memory, like seeing the city from an airplane, he sees life as a whole. The hard places are not as visible, the pain and suffering is quieted, and the entire panorama is beautiful and inspiring. It is good to sing the hymn:

> When upon life's billows you are tempest tossed,
> When you are discouraged, thinking all is lost,
> Count your many blessings, name them one by one,
> And it will surprise you what the Lord hath done.
>
> E. O. EXCELL

Forget not the works of God—remember. Memory and hope are very closely connected. We use the same faculties to look both backward and forward. If we look back and see the works of God, we will be inspired to look into the future and believe there are blessings ahead. We will be inspired to "keep his commandments" if we believe that faithfulness and service will not go unrewarded.

Saint Paul declares confidently, "The sufferings of this present time are not worthy to be compared with the glory which shall be revealed in us" (Romans 8:18). This is a marvelous hope, but how can he be so sure? He says, "We know that all things work together for good to them that love God ..." (verse 28). This has been proven by his own experience and observation. He can look back at life and see that it has worked out well. He can see this because he is looking at the total experience of life instead of one incident or moment. Because he can get the distant view of life backward, he can also get the distant view of life forward. He sees glory ahead.

He Leadeth Me

In pastures green? Not always; sometimes He
Who knoweth best, in kindness leadeth me
In weary ways, where heavy shadows be—

Out of the sunshine warm and soft and bright,
Out of the sunshine into darkest night;
I oft would faint with sorrow and affright—

Only for this—I know He holds my hand,
So whether in the green or desert land,
I trust, although I may not understand.

And by still waters? No, not always so;
Ofttimes the heavy tempests round me blow,
And o'er my soul the waves and billows go.

But when the storms beat loudest, and I cry
Aloud for help, the Master standeth by,
And whispers to my soul, "Lo, it is I."

Above the tempest wild I hear Him say,
"Beyond this darkness lies the perfect day,
In every path of thine I lead the way."

So, whether on the hill-tops high and fair
I dwell, or in the sunless valleys where
The shadows lie—what matter? He is there.

And more than this; where'er the pathway lead
He gives to me no helpless, broken reed,
But His own hand, sufficient for my need.

So where He leads me I can safely go;
And in the blest hereafter I shall know
Why in His wisdom He hath led me so.

7.

... hope thou in God.

This is the greatest statement on hope in the Bible. It sums it all up. One of the Ten Commandments is: "Thou shalt not take the name of the LORD thy God in vain . . ." (Exodus 20:7). Often that has been interpreted as meaning using God's name as profanity. But sometimes our swearwords are more stupid than sinful. The most profane word in the English language is the word "hopeless." To proclaim hopelessness is to deny the presence and power of God.

Time after time man has expressed hopelessness. In 1801 Wilberforce said that he dared not marry because the future was too unsettled. In 1806 William Penn said, "There is scarcely anything around us but ruin and despair." In 1848 Lord Shaftsbury said, "Nothing can save the British Empire from shipwreck." In 1849 Benjamin Disraeli said, "In industry, commerce, and agriculture there is no hope." In 1852 the dying Duke of Wellington said, "I thank God that I shall be spared from seeing the consummation of ruin that is settling in around us." In 1914 Lord Grey said, "The lamps are going out all over Europe; we shall not see them lit again in our lifetime."

We read and hear such expressions as these over and

over. There are many who see no brightness in the future. To them all the good is past. Almost twenty thousand people a year commit suicide in the United States. They have lost all hope.

The Psalmist asked, "Why art thou cast down, O my soul? and why art thou disquieted in me?" (Psalms 42:5). There are as many answers to that question as there are people. My own observation leads me to believe that the chief cause of discouragement and despair is loneliness.

In his play *Orpheus Descending,* Tennessee Williams has one of the characters say a gloomy thing: "We're all of us sentenced to solitary confinement inside our own skins for life! . . . we got to face it, we're under a life-long sentence to solitary confinement inside our own lonely skins for as long as we live on this earth!"

One of the characters in *The Cocktail Party* by T. S. Eliot says much the same thing:

> What is hell? Hell is oneself,
> Hell is alone . . . . There is nothing to escape from
> And nothing to escape to. One is always alone.

Or one could turn to another play which is entitled *When Ladies Meet,* written by Rachel Crothers. One of the characters says that he hasn't found anything, except to know that he hasn't got anything that really counts. Nobody belongs to him—nobody whose very existence depends on him. He is completely and absolutely alone.

As the minister of a church located in the center of Houston, numbering almost eleven thousand members, I see daily the problems of people. Loneliness is the problem I see the most. There is the loneliness of those who are old and sick and often forgotten. There is the loneliness of one cut off from a loved one by death. There is the loneliness of a youth whose parents cannot communicate with him. There are many types of lonely people. Loneliness in a crowded city seems to be the worst. Loneliness is different from being alone. It is different from solitude. Loneliness is the feeling of being isolated from others.

When the Psalmist said to himself, "Why art thou cast down," it is very likely it was because of loneliness, because he then says, "hope thou in God." There is One who is always near and available. If one really believes in God, he never lacks strengthening companionship. Faith in, and fellowship with God overcomes our feelings of hopelessness.

W. Albert Donaldson, in *You Can Hope Again*, tells about a party of tourists who went to Lick Observatory to view the heavens. As they looked through the great telescope, an astronomer said, "You will see a cluster of stars called Hercules, which is the finest in the northern sky. You can count six thousand or more stars. Each star is a sun, and each one you see is probably larger than our sun. Probably each sun has planets, and there are possibly moons around each planet, and there may be life, both plant and animal, on these planets."

After coming down from the observation chair, one of the visitors said, "Did you say all those stars are suns?"

"Yes."

"Did you say they are all larger than our sun?"

"Yes."

"Can you tell how large our sun is?"

"Well," said the astronomer, "if the sun were a hollow shell, you could pour over a million earths into it, and there would still be much space left."

The visitor was lost in contemplation for a brief minute, and then he said, "Well, then I guess it doesn't matter what happens to us in the coming election."

When we think of the greatness of God, it overcomes our feelings of helplessness and defeat. We are not lonely. Sidney Lanier was striken with tuberculosis. He felt deserted and defeated. One day he sat looking at the marsh on the coast of Georgia. He was moved to write:

> As the marsh-hen secretly builds on the watery sod,
> Behold I will build me a nest in the greatness of God.

I have read over and over a passage written by Ernest Hemingway in "A Natural History of the Dead":

> When that persevering traveller, Mungo Park, was at one period of his course fainting in the vast wilderness of an African desert, naked and alone,

considering his days as numbered and nothing ap-
pearing to remain for him to do but to lie down
and die, a small moss-flower of extraordinary beauty
caught his eye. "Though the whole plant," says he,
"was no larger than one of my fingers, I could not
contemplate the delicate confirmation of its roots,
leaves and capsules without admiration. Can that Being
who planted, watered and brought to perfection, in
this obscure part of the world, a thing which appears
of so small importance, look with unconcern upon the
situation and suffering of creatures formed after his
own image? Surely not. Reflections like these would
not allow me to despair; I started up and, disregarding
both hunger and fatigue, travelled forward, assured
that relief was at hand; and I was not disappointed."

Jesus told us that God is a father. To some people
there is no inspiration in thinking thus. Fathers can be
cruel, disappointing, unloving. We have all heard stories
of children's hearts being broken at Christmas because
of some unworthy father. A family of children went
to bed on Christmas Eve, excitedly anticipating their
presents the next morning. The father had gone to
town that day with the list of toys to buy. Late that
night he came home drunk. He had spent all his money
and had completely forgotten the children. Now all
the shops were closed.

Eagerly the children got up on Christmas morning

and ran to see the presents, but their stockings were empty. There was nothing. Tears of disappointment flowed down their cheeks. They had every reason to hope except for the fact that the one upon whom their hopes were based proved to be untrustworthy.

The Psalmist said, ". . . the judgments of the LORD are true and righteous altogether" (Psalms 19:9). Many of us have experienced moments when we may have doubted this. Many afternoons my wife and I have driven to the edge of our city and turned into a lovely cemetery. We wind our way through that cemetery and stop. We get out and stand by 'two tiny graves. They are the graves of two little grandsons of ours. With great joy did we anticipate the birth of each of them. How we looked forward to playing with and loving those little boys. I prayed with all the faith I had for them. I asked God to let them live. Instead we buried them. I know about hurt and disappointment.

I have also lived long enough to know that one cannot judge the character of God based on the tragedies of this life. Leslie D. Weatherhead wrote a little book entitled *The Will of God*. It explains it better than anything else I have ever read. He talks about the intentional will of God, the circumstantial will of God, and the ultimate will of God. Sometimes things happen which God does not intend. Sometimes God allows things to happen under the circumstances. But ultimately God's will triumphs. We sing:

Not now, but in the coming years,
It may be in a better land,
We'll read the meaning of our tears,
And there, sometime, we'll understand.

MAXWELL N. CORNELIUS

Saint Paul said, "Now we see through a glass, darkly. . ." (1 Corinthians 13:12). We do not understand so many things and we hope that the things which happen which we think are the worst, someday we will realize were the best. I gain strength from these words: "Behold, the eye of the LORD is on those who fear him, on those who hope in his steadfast love" (Psalms 33:18 RSV). Sometimes we trust God "on account of." Other times we trust God "in spite of." We sing:

Come, ye disconsolate, where'er ye languish,
Come to the mercy seat, fervently kneel;
Here bring your wounded hearts, here tell your anguish;
Earth has no sorrows that heaven cannot heal.

THOMAS MOORE

If there were no God who ruled over this universe, if there were no heavenly Father who watched over mankind, then hope would be an illusion. With no God, the world would be like a ship with no one in command, drifting aimlessly on the sea. But through all of life there is a guiding hand. There is one everlasting reason for hope—"hope thou in God."

Some of man's suffering comes through ignorance. Many children died because of diphtheria; many have gone through life crippled because of polio. But we found a preventative for these and many other things that have hurt people. We have hope that we will find the cure for cancer and for so many other things that have brought despair. This hope is what builds hospitals and supports vast research programs.

Men suffer because of the brutality of other men. Children are mistreated by brutal parents, minorities are trampled by bigots, killing and destruction is brought about by wars. The list could go on and on. But we still cling to the hope that men can learn to live together in love and that hope causes those of goodwill to keep trying.

Wickedness is not hopeless. Jonathan Edwards's sermon "Sinners in the Hands of an Angry God" typifies the preaching and thinking of a lot of people—if one does wrong, to hell with him. But Jesus came to call sinners to repentance (Matthew 9:13). There is hope for every sinner. Robert Burns, the beloved Scotch poet, wrote a poem to the devil in which he had the audacity to hope that even Satan might be converted. There is hope for the worst sinners among us. There is hope for you and for me—no matter what sins we have committed and no matter how guilty we now feel. That is why we build churches and keep on preaching the gospel.

8.

I have hoped in thy word.

On every page of the Bible there are words of God that give reason for hope. Sometimes when I feel a bit discouraged, I begin reading some of the promises of God, while remembering a little verse:

> He has never broken
> Any promise ever spoken.

In the promises of God I find inspiration and new hope. Here let me tell of half a dozen promises which lift me up. If space permitted, I could list hundreds more.

". . . Whosoever believeth in him should not perish, but have everlasting life" (John 3:16). That is the greatest promise of all. "Whosoever" includes me. This means that in spite of my own unworthiness, because I believe in Christ I am not doomed. I hope for eternity. I can face death without fear.

"If ye ask any thing in my name, I will do it" (John 14:14). That is almost too good to be true. Of course, I know that to ask in His name is serious business. It means I must be dedicated to His plans and purposes. But I am promised that if I am sincerely committed to Christ, I can pray and my prayer will be granted.

"In the world ye shall have tribulation: but be of good cheer; I have overcome the world" (John 16:33). Tribulations in this world are many—sickness, poverty, handicaps, disappointments, and on and on the list goes. But in the midst of tribulations I can be a cheerful person because of the assurance that our Lord overcomes all of these.

"Blessed is the man that walketh not in the counsel of the ungodly . . . he shall be like a tree planted by the rivers of water, that bringeth forth his fruit in his season; his leaf also shall not wither; and whatsoever he doeth shall prosper" (Psalms 1:1, 3). A sense of failure will sooner or later come to every person. We dream and work but sometimes we do not seem to accomplish very much. We begin to wonder if our lives are worthwhile and if the efforts we have made really amount to anything. But we have the promise that if we are faithful, our lives will be fruitful and we will not end up as failures.

"Lo, I am with you alway . . ." (Matthew 28:20). I like the story of the Chinese man whose name was Lo. He had become a Christian and was reading the New Testament for the first time. When he got to the last verse in Saint Matthew he became very excited. He told a friend, "The Lord Jesus wrote this for me because He said, "Lo, I am with you alway." And he was correct. The Lord was speaking to him and to each and every one of us.

"If ye have faith as a grain of mustard seed, ye shall say unto this mountain, Remove hence to yonder place; and it shall remove; and nothing shall be impossible unto you" (Matthew 17:20). A full-grown and complete faith is not required. A mustard seed is very small. If one has only a little faith, like the seed, it can grow and can overcome the mountain of any difficulty. This means that we need not be defeated.

There truly is hope in God's Word. Often I come in at night after some engagement and before going to bed, I sit down for awhile and read the newspaper or watch the news on television. Much of the news is bad. It tells of the troubles people have suffered that day. If one only fills his mind with the happenings of today, he will have a tendency toward despair. So it is very important to also read some of the eternal words of God in order to balance our thinking.

9.

**In hope of eternal life, which God, that
cannot lie, promised before the world began.**

On every page of the Bible there is a word to assure
man that life on this earth is not all there is to know.

"The righteous hath hope in his death" (Proverbs
14:32).

"Today shalt thou be with me in paradise" (Luke
23:43).

"I am the resurrection, and the life: he that believeth
in me. . . . shall never die" (John 11:25, 26).

"For we know that if our earthly house of this
tabernacle were dissolved, we have a building of God,
an house not made with hands, eternal in the heavens"
(2 Corinthians 5:1).

"If in this life only we have hope in Christ, we are
of all men most miserable" (1 Corinthians 15:19).

"And God shall wipe away all tears from their
eyes; and there shall be no more death . . ." (Revelation
21:4).

The hope of life beyond this life has given so very
many the strength to bear great suffering and toil. The
old Negro slave had very little to look forward to on
this earth. But he could keep going because he had a

firm hope which enabled him to sing such songs as:

> I looked over Jordan, and what did I see,
> Coming for to carry me home?
> A band of angels a-comin' after me,
> Coming for to carry me home.

There were those early pioneers in our land who battled the hardships of the frontier. The winters were cold, the work was hard, they had almost no defense against sickness. In those days people died at an early age. But they kept going and one of their inspirations was to go to some little frame church on the Lord's day and sing:

> There's a land that is fairer than day,
> And by faith we can see it afar;
> For the Father waits over the way,
> To prepare us a dwelling place there.
>
> *In the sweet by and by,*
> *We shall meet on that beautiful shore.*

S. F. BENNETT

Fanny Crosby was blind from the time she was a baby. She wrote many wonderful songs, but perhaps her best was the one written out of hope of eternal life. She sang:

> But O, the joy when I shall wake
> Within the palace of the King!
>
> *And I shall see Him face to face.*

There are those who belittle the songs which look
forward to the next life. They would like to take
out of our songbooks such songs as "When the Roll Is
Called Up Yonder," "On Jordan's Stormy Banks I
Stand," "When They Ring Those Golden Bells," and
others. There are those who say such songs are merely
escapist—that these songs merely look forward to
deliverance from the world and its troubles instead of
facing responsibly the problems of the world. But such
is not the case. The hope of life beyond this life is the
inspiration to man to live nobly and sacrificially in this
life. If life on this earth were all there were, many would
question that it is worth the struggle. The assurance of
life eternal gives strength and meaning and purpose to
the sufferings and struggles of this life. Hope of eternity
causes us to want to do our best in the here and now.

C. S. Lewis said it well in *Christian Behavior:*

Hope is one of the Theological virtues. This means
that a continual looking forward to the eternal world
is not (as some modern people think) a form of
escapism or wishful thinking, but one of the things a
Christian is meant to do. It does not mean that we are
to leave the present world as it is. If you read history

you will find that the Christians who did most for
the present world were just those who thought most
of the next. The Apostles themselves, who set on foot
the conversion of the Roman Empire, the great men
who built up the Middle Ages, the English Evangelicals
who abolished the Slave Trade, all left their mark on
Earth, precisely because their minds were occupied
with Heaven. It is since Christians have largely ceased
to think of the other world that they have become so
ineffective in this. Aim at Heaven and you will get
earth "thrown in": aim at earth and you will get
neither.

There is an eternal struggle between life and death,
between hope and despair. For us who are Christians,
this struggle is best symbolized in the Easter story.
Christ's followers had watched Him die and had seen
Him buried in a tomb sealed with a large stone.
Their world had crashed. Now they were frightened,
purposeless people. But not all of those who loved Him
were entirely without hope. In Saint Mark's story we
read one of the most inspiring verses in the whole Bible:
"And very early in the morning, the first day of the
week, they came unto the sepulchre at the rising of the
sun" (Mark 16:2). They knew a heavy stone sealed that
sepulchre and they did ask who would roll away the
stone, but in the act of coming and in asking that
question they were expressing their hope. They had not

surrendered. In their minds they believed that somehow the stone could be rolled away. These faithful women had not surrendered to defeat. They did not expect the Resurrection, but at least they could anoint His body.

Those people who possess hope are never seeking an easy way out. They are not the ones who run away from the problems of their lives and their world. They are the ones who keep on believing that solutions can be found, that stones can be rolled away.

We can look at our world and see many stones in the way. There are some who are mere head-shakers or hand-wringers. They talk about how bad everything is and they see ahead only doom and destruction. But the hopeful persons in this life see "the rising of the sun" and are up and about on some important mission.

10.

Blessed be the God and Father of our Lord Jesus Christ, which according to his abundant mercy hath begotten us again unto a lively hope by the resurrection of Jesus Christ from the dead.

The Resurrection of Jesus Christ is God's mightiest act. This is what literally created the Christian faith and is the ground of Christian hope. The noun *hope* does not appear in the four Gospels. Nowhere is Jesus quoted as using the word hope. For those who wrote the Gospels, hope was born with the Resurrection. Saint Paul and the other New Testament writers use the word hope often. Christ is alive and on that fact Christian hope is founded.

The Resurrection of Christ means far more than the mere resuscitation of a dead body. There are numerous stories of bodies which have been brought back to life. We remember that Elisha revived the dead son of a widow from Shunem (2 Kings 4:32-37). Jesus raised the dead daughter of Jairus (Mark 5:21-43). Also, Jesus brought back to life the son of the widow from Nain (Luke 7:11-16). Lazarus lay four days in the tomb before Jesus raised him back to life (John 11:17). We have read more than one newspaper story of a dead body coming back to life. This is not the main point of the

56

Resurrection. In fact, Saint Paul never mentions the empty tomb.

The Resurrection of Christ was God's final designation of Him as His own Son. Saint Paul says, ". . . Jesus Christ . . . declared to be the Son of God with power . . . by the resurrection from the dead" (Romans 1:3, 4). Also, Saint Paul speaks of "the power of his resurrection" (Philippians 3:10). That means that through Christ a life can be transformed, can be saved now and forever. This is man's greatest hope. It means that man has hope both in this life and in the life to come.

Eternal life assures us of more than the mere survival of our souls. It means more than the continuation of life as we now know it. It affirms the fact that God will bring to completion His purposes for each of His children. Death cannot defeat God's plan for any one of us.

Certainly Christ gives hope to every one of us for this life. Let me quote here a poem that beautifully expresses our earthly hopes in Him:

The Miracle Dreams

That night when in Judean skies
    The mystic star dispensed her light,
A blind man moved amid his sleep,
    And dreamed that he had sight.

That night when shepherds heard the song
  Of hosts angelic choiring near,
A deaf man stirred in slumber's spell
  And dreamed that he could hear.

That night when in the cattle stall
  Slept child and mother cheek by jowl,
A cripple turned his twisted limbs,
  And dreamed that he was whole.

That night when o'er the new-born babe
  The tender Mary rose to lean,
A loathsome leper smiled in sleep,
  And dreamed that he was clean.

That night when to the mother's breast
  The little King was held secure,
A harlot slept a happy sleep,
  And dreamed that she was pure.

That night when in a manger lay
  The Sanctified who came to save,
A man moved in the sleep of death,
  And dreamed there was no grave.

                              SUSIE M. BEST

Not only "that night" but every night since He came, people have dreamed with new hope. Christ did not need to talk about hope. He was and He is the hope of every person and of the world. We rightly sing:

> My hope is built on nothing less
> Than Jesus' blood and righteousness.

EDWARD MOTE

Christ is our hope not only in this life, but beyond this life. "If in this life only we have hope in Christ, we are of all men most miserable," said Saint Paul (1 Corinthians 15:19).

11.
Thy kingdom come. Thy will be done
in earth, as it is in heaven.

What a glorious hope that prayer of our Lord expresses for our world! There are those who can only see the world getting worse and worse.. On every side we hear predictions of doom and destruction. We do not blind our eyes to the ills and wrongs of our society. There is so much in our world that is wrong. But neither do we surrender in defeat. If we can only believe that this creation is going to be abolished, then we must conclude that Christianity has nothing to offer man in his present predicament.

In the Book of Zechariah we read a thrilling challenge: "Return to your stronghold, O prisoners of hope . . ." (9:12 RSV). This was written during dismal, disappointing times. The holy city lay in ruin. The temple was destroyed. The people had been conquered and were downcast and afraid. Their voices were reduced to mere whispers or to silence. But the prophet shouts a clarion call: "Return to your stronghold." He tells them that they are not prisoners of defeat, or of helplessness, or of evil conquerors. He declares they are "prisoners of hope."

Being conquered and bound by hope, they are

compelled to rise and face, in the language of Paul, their "heavenly vision." They are called to courage instead of fear; to sacrifice instead of surrender; to action instead of silence. Being "prisoners of hope," they cannot look at their world, as bad as it is, with hopelessness.

Truly, every Christian is, as Paul said of himself, "the prisoner of Jesus Christ" (Ephesians 3:1). Because He is the hope of the world, it therefore must follow that Christ's prisoners are "prisoners of hope." Christians believe that God cares about His world and is working with men to bring His kingdom on earth. At times progress seems mighty slow and it seems some of the time that wrong is on the throne. But we who are bound by hope must always believe:

> And behind the dim unknown,
> Standeth God within the shadow,
> Keeping watch above his own.

JAMES RUSSELL LOWELL

This hope compels us to keep working at our task of giving all we have in Christ's service. "God so loved the world, that he gave his only begotten son ..." (John 3:16). Jesus came bringing a message of peace, righteousness, and love. He gave to the world a hope that is both beautiful and transforming. We cannot believe that God will allow His Son's mission to fail. Because of our hope, we sing, "The Kingdom

Is Coming," and we give ourselves to that end.

> I live for those who love me,
>   For those who know me true,
> For the heaven that smiles above me,
>   And awaits my spirit too;
> For the cause that lacks assistance,
>   For the wrong that needs resistance,
> For the future in the distance,
>   And the good that I can do.

GEORGE LINNAEUS BANKS

12.

And now abideth . . . hope.

Underscore that word "abideth." It is a sturdy word. It is regretful that the word hope has become weakened in our language. For many, hope has come to mean mere wishful thinking. "I hope it won't rain tomorrow," we say. But hope is a strong soldier which marches side by side with the great words faith and love. Saint Paul bids us to "Put on the whole armour of God." He assures us that clothed with God's armor we can successfully contend against "the rulers of the darkness of this world," that we can face up to evil and keep standing. He lists the various parts of God's armor and he refers to the "helmet of salvation" (Ephesians 6:11-17). In another place the apostle tells us that the helmet is "the hope of salvation" (1 Thessalonians 5:8). Hope is strong enough to be included as part of God's armor.

No matter what happens, the Christian believes there is always a future. Hope causes us to realize there is always something ahead. Hope will have nothing to do with that defeatest nonsense—that there will always be wars, that man will always be selfish and sinful, that hunger and poverty can never be overcome. Hope is so sturdy, so real, and so aggressive that no matter what enemy it faces it does not back down—it "abideth."

Saint Paul tested hope in the burning fires of experience. He faced enough to shake the confidence of anybody, yet he found that in spite of every persecution, sickness, disappointment, and seeming defeat, hope still met the test. Nothing could destroy hope. "And now abideth . . . hope," he declared.

About sixteen centuries after Paul lived, a boy was born in Britain. Early in life he was stricken by a disease which grotesquely crippled him for life. Despite his suffering and handicaps, Alexander Pope came to be regarded by his generation as the greatest of English poets. This man who knew lifelong suffering wrote:

Hope springs eternal in the human breast.